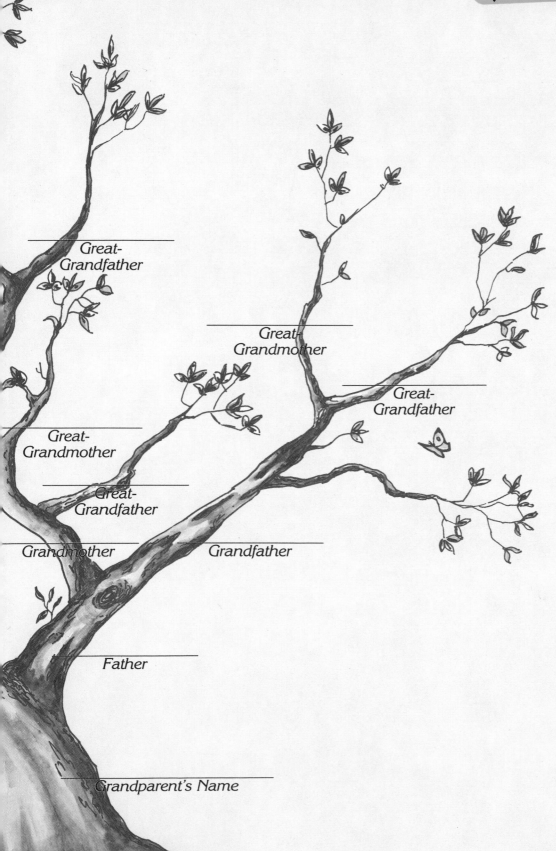

Great-
Grandfather

Great-
Grandmother

Great-
Grandfather

Great-
Grandmother

Great-
Grandfather

Grandmother

Grandfather

Father

Grandparent's Name

# A Grandparents Book

by

_____

*(Grandparent's name)*

_____

*(Date of birth)*

_____

*(Place of birth)*

Dear Gramma Sweet,

Here is a present for you
which I hope to read someday!
Love,
David Andrew
( My first Christmas, Dec. 25, 1990)

# ANSWERS TO
# A GRANDCHILD'S
# QUESTIONS

## A Grandparents Book

## Milton Kamen

**HPBooks**
a division of
PRICE STERN SLOAN
Los Angeles

Published by HPBooks
A division of Price Stern Sloan, Inc.
360 North La Cienega Boulevard
Los Angeles, CA 90048

Printed in U.S.A.
Revised Edition
9 8 7 6 5

# Contents

# A Grandparents Book

# Note to a Grandparent

## *Congratulations!*

*You are about to begin an adventure in nostalgia. When you complete this book, it will contain information about you that your grandchild will someday consider priceless. By writing your direct, simple answers to the questions asked, you will create a lasting history of yourself and your family.*

*When your grandchildren know and understand your life story, they will better understand who they are and how they got where they are—their heritage, their background and their roots.*

*Thoughtful and careful answers to the questions will help you and your grandchild enjoy the pleasant memories of the past. You may prefer to draft your answers on scrap paper before entering them into this permanent record.*

*Note that questions in the book are written as if the grandchild were asking them directly of you. Try to include as many dates as you can. If some questions are not applicable, skip them or cross them out and use the space for other information and memories you would like to record. Be sure to enter your name on the first page!*

*This book will help you create a work of self-expression—a most personal and unique gift for your grandchild to treasure forever!*

# Beginnings

# Beginnings

*Where were you born?*
    *(City or town, state, country)*

_____

_____


*What was the month, day and year?*
    *What time was it?*

_____

_____


*How much did you weigh at birth?*
    *Were you a healthy new-born baby?*

_____

_____


*What were your parents' names?*
    *How old were they?*

_____

_____

_____

_____


*Notes:*

## Beginnings

*Where were you when I was born?*

*Did you predict correctly
 whether I would be a boy or girl?*

*How did you find out I had arrived?*

*Who were the first people you told?*

*Did you suggest a name,
 or names, for me?*

*When and where was the first time
 you saw me?*

*Notes:*

# Beginnings

*Was there anything unusual about
the circumstances of your birth?*

*What was your full name?*

*Does your name have a special
meaning?*

*Notes:*

# When You Were Very Young

*A Grandparents Book*

# When You Were Very Young

*Where is the first home you remember?*
  *What did it look like?*

_____

_____

_____

*Who were your neighbors?*

_____

_____

_____

*Who was your first "best friend"?*

_____

_____

*Who were your other friends?*

_____

_____

*Do you still have any favorite things*
  *that you had as a child?*

_____

_____

_____

*Notes:*

# When You Were Very Young

*Did you have brothers/sisters when*
*you were very young? When were they born?*

*What do you remember about your*
*room?*

*What were your favorite toys?*

*What were your favorite games?*

*What is the first present*
*you remember giving? To Whom?*

*Notes:*

# When You Were Very Young

*What is the first present you*
*remember receiving?*

*What was your favorite book?*

*Did you have favorite stories?*

*Did you have a secret hiding place?*

*Notes:*

# When You Were Very Young

*Did your family have any pets?*

*What kind?*

*What were their names?*

*Did you have favorite relatives?*

*Did you have a nickname?*

*How did you get it?*

*Did you like or dislike it?*

*Notes:*

## When You Were Very Young

*Who took care of you if your*
*parents were away?*

*Did you have a grown-up friend*
*who was not a relative?*

*What was the first movie you saw?*

*Notes:*

# When You Were Very Young

*What were your favorite radio programs?*

_____

_____

_____

*What were your favorite TV programs?*

_____

_____

_____

*What indoor games did you play?*

_____

_____

*What outdoor games did you play?*

_____

_____

*Who did you play with?*

_____

_____

_____

*Notes:*

# When You Were Very Young

*Is there one special early memory
    you have of your mother?*

*Is there one special early memory
    you have of your father?*

*Notes:*

# Growing Up

# Growing Up: Grammar School Years

*What grammar school did you go to?*
*Where was it?*

*When did you attend?*

*Who were your favorite teachers?*
*What was special about them?*

*What were your favorite*
*grammar school subjects?*

*Were you in any school plays*
*or concerts?*

*What did you do after school?*

*Notes:*

## Growing Up: Grammar School Years

*Who were your best friends
in grammar school?*

*How late did you stay up during
school nights?*

*What chores did you have at home?*

*Notes:*

## Growing Up: Grammar School Years

*What do you remember about
   your summer vacations?*

*What do you remember about
   the school buildings?*

*Did you get an allowance?*

*How did you spend it?*

*Notes:*

# Growing Up: High School Years

*What high school did you go to?*
    *Where was it?*

_____

_____

_____

*Who were your favorite high school teachers?*
    *What was special about them?*

_____

_____

_____

_____

*Who were the teachers you didn't*
    *like? What do you remember about them?*

_____

_____

_____

*What were your favorite*
    *high school subjects?*

_____

_____

_____

_____

*Notes:*

# Growing Up: High School Years

*What subjects did you dislike?*

*Who were your closest friends?*

*What were your favorite sports?*

*Were you on any school teams?*

*Notes:*

# Growing Up: High School Years

*Did you belong to any clubs?*
*What were they?*

_____

_____

*Were you involved in any activities*
*—i.e. newspaper, scholastic clubs, etc.?*

_____

_____

*Did you win any academic, social*
*or athletic awards or prizes?*

_____

_____

_____

*Who was the most envied person*
*in your school? Why?*

_____

_____

_____

*Notes:*

# Growing Up: High School Years

*What teacher influenced you the most?*

*Who did you date?*

*Was there someone you wanted to
date but never did?*

*What did you want to be or do when
you were finished with high school?*

*Notes:*

# Growing Up: High School Years

*What friends had the most influence*
*on you?*

_____

_____

*Did you fight with anyone? Who was*
*it and what did you fight over?*

_____

_____

_____

*Did you have any part-time jobs*
*during the school year?*

_____

_____

*How much money did you earn?*

_____

_____

_____

*Notes:*

## Growing Up: High School Years

*What did you like best about*
*summer vacations?*

*Did you ever work during summer*
*vacations? What did you do?*

*How much did you earn?*

*What were your favorite books?*

*What were your favorite movies?*

*Notes:*

# Growing Up: High School Years

*Who were your favorite athletes?*

_____

_____

_____

*What magazines did you read?*

_____

_____

_____

_____

*What television or radio programs did*
*you follow?*

_____

_____

_____

*Who were your favorite actors or*
*actresses?*

_____

_____

_____

_____

*Notes:*

## Growing Up: High School Years

*What were the most popular songs?*

*What dances did you do?*

*What were your favorite clothes?*

*What were the major clothing fads?*

*Notes:*

## Growing Up: High School Years

*What were the most popular slang
    terms and phrases?*

*What did you do in high school that
    gave you the most satisfaction?*

*What was the greatest disappointment
    you experienced?*

*Did you drive a car?*

*Notes:*

# Growing Up: High School Years

*Who taught you how to drive?*

*What kind of car did you drive?*

*How did you get along with
    your mother?*

*How did you get along with
    your father?*

*Notes:*

## Growing Up: High School Years

*Who were the adults you considered
    friends?*

*What were your neighbors like?*

*Who did you have "crushes" on?*

*Did you fall in love with anyone?*

*Notes:*

# Growing Up: College, University Years

*Did you go to college?*
*Where was it?*

*What was your major course of study?*

*Did you have any outstanding or*
*memorable teachers?*

*What were your goals when you were*
*a student?*

*Were you involved in any extra-*
*curricular activities?*

*Notes:*

# Growing Up: College, University Years

*Were you a member of any clubs?*

*What were your most important
    learning experiences?*

*What kind of a student were you?*

*Did you receive any awards,
    prizes, or degrees?*

*What do you remember best?*

*Notes:*

# Growing Up: College, University Years

*Did you attend any graduate
or professional schools? Why?*

*What did you study?*

*Did you receive any awards,
prizes, or degrees?*

*Who were your closest
friends and roommates?*

*What do you remember best?*

*Notes:*

# Friends

## Friends

*What friends have you stayed in touch*
*with since childhood?*

*What friends have you stayed in touch*
*with since your teen years?*

*What friends have surprised you by*
*getting in touch?*

*What friends have you meant to keep*
*in touch with, but haven't?*

*What friendships have you renewed?*

*Notes:*

# Friends

*Who are your closest friends now?*
*How did you meet them?*

_____

_____

_____

*What recent acquaintances have*
*become friends?*

_____

_____

_____

*Have you ever gone to a reunion? Which?*
*What was it like? How did you react?*

_____

_____

_____

_____

*Notes:*

# Friends

*Do you have any friends who became famous?*

*What is the strangest place you ever
     began a friendship?*

*Who is your most amusing friend?*

*Have you ever had a serious quarrel
     with a friend? What happened?*

*Notes:*

# Friends

*Where and when did you meet your husband's/wife's best friend?*

_____

_____

_____

*What is your favorite story about any of your friends?*

_____

_____

_____

_____

*Who, within the family, has been your best friend?*

_____

_____

_____

*Notes:*

# Friends

*What friends have done, or would do,
     the most for you without being asked?*

*Have you done things for friends with-
     out them knowing it? What? When?*

*What do you most value in a friendship?*

*Who is the best friend you've ever had?*

*Notes:*

# At Your
# Own Home

# At Your Own Home

*When did you leave your parents' home?*
*Why and where did you move?*

_____

_____

_____

*How much rent did you pay?*

_____

_____

*What did your home look like?*
*How large was it? How was it furnished?*

_____

_____

_____

_____

*How long did you live there?*
*Why did you next move? Where?*

_____

_____

_____

*Notes:*

## At Your Own Home

*How many other houses or apartments
have you lived in?*

*What were your addresses? When were
you there?*

*Do you have any furnishings that
belonged to your parents?*

*Notes:*

# At Your Own Home

*What is the least expensive home or*
*apartment you've ever had?*

_____

_____

_____

*What is the most expensive?*

_____

_____

_____

*Which homes or apartments have you*
*enjoyed the most? Why?*

_____

_____

_____

_____

_____

_____

_____

*Notes:*

## At Your Own Home

*What room have you liked the best*
*in any of your homes?*

*What have been your favorite pieces*
*of furniture?*

Notes:

# At Your Own Home

*Who have been your favorite neighbors?*

_____

_____

_____

_____

_____

_____

*Who have been the most irritating neighbors?*

_____

_____

_____

_____

_____

_____

*Notes:*

# Marriage

*A Grandparents Book*

# Marriage

*How did you meet my grandfather/*
*grandmother?*

*How old were you?*
*How old was he/she?*

*What attracted you to each other?*

*How long did you know each other*
*before you discussed marriage?*

*How did you become engaged?*

*Notes:*

# Marriage

*How did your parents react when*
*you told them?*

_____

_____

_____

*How did his/her parents react when*
*you told them?*

_____

_____

_____

_____

*What do you remember most about*
*your courtship?*

_____

_____

_____

_____

*What ring or token did you give or*
*receive as an engagement present?*

_____

_____

_____

*Notes:*

# Marriage

*When and where were you married?*

*What did you wear?*

*Who was at your wedding?*

*What do you remember best about the
ceremony?*

*Notes:*

## Marriage

*Where did you spend the first night
of your marriage?*

*Did you receive wedding presents?
What were they?*

*Do you have photographs of your
wedding? Where are they?*

*Did you go on a honeymoon? Where?
How long?*

*Notes:*

# Marriage

*What were the first things you bought together for your home?*

*What surprised you most about my grandfather/grandmother after you married?*

*What was the first argument you had after the wedding?*

*Notes:*

# Marriage

*What friends have you seen most as*
*a couple?*

*What has he/she done that has made*
*you proud?*

*What pastimes, games, sports or*
*leisure interests do you share?*

*Have you and your husband/wife enjoyed*
*good health? If not, what were the problems?*

*Notes:*

# Marriage

*What is your favorite story about
my grandmother/grandfather?*

*Did you marry more than once?
Whom?*

*Did you have children by another
marriage?*

*Notes:*

# Travel

## Travel

*How old were you when you took your first trip?*
*Where did you go? How did you travel?*

*Which childhood trip do you remember*
*most vividly? Why?*

*When did you take your first plane*
*ride? Were you scared?*

*Did you or your parents take photographs of your*
*trips? Do you still have any?*

*Notes:*

# Travel

*Do you remember the first hotel
    you stayed in? Which one? When?*

*What is the most adventurous thing
    that occurred while you were travelling?*

*What is the funniest thing that ever
    happened to you during a trip?*

*Notes:*

## Travel

*Were you ever lost while travelling?*

*Were you ever in need of a Good Samaritan on a trip? Did you find one?*

*Have you had any health problems while travelling?*

*Where did you go on your first trip with your husband/wife?*

*Notes:*

## Travel

*What is the most exotic or extra-*
*ordinary trip you've taken?*

_____

_____

_____

_____

_____

_____

_____

_____

*What is the strangest mode of trans-*
*portation you've used while on a trip?*

_____

_____

_____

_____

*Notes:*

# Travel

*What is the best trip the two of you have taken together?*

_____

_____

_____

_____

_____

_____

*Do you have any purchases or mementos from your travels?*

_____

_____

_____

_____

_____

*Notes:*

## Travel

*Have you ever travelled with friends?
When? With whom? Where did you go?*

*Have you made any friends while travelling? When and how?*

*What foreign countries have you travelled to?*

*Notes:*

# Travel

*What places would you return to?*

_____

_____

_____

_____

_____

*What places would you not return to?*

_____

_____

_____

_____

*Have you ever taken a cruise?*
    *What ship? How long was the trip?*

_____

_____

_____

_____

*Notes:*

# Travel

*What is the best hotel you stayed in? Why?*

*What is the best restaurant you've eaten in while travelling?*

*Notes:*

# Travel

*What is the most spectacular sight*
*you've seen while travelling?*

*What is the single greatest memory*
*you have of a trip you've taken?*

*Notes:*

# Work, Jobs, Money

# Work, Jobs, Money

*What was your first full-time job? How much did you earn? What were your responsibilities?*

*Describe your first boss.*

*What has been your main occupation? Why did you choose it? How did you get started?*

*For whom have you worked?*

*Notes:*

# Work, Jobs, Money

*What other jobs have you had?*

_____

_____

_____

_____

_____

*What is the most important promotion you've received?*

_____

_____

_____

_____

*What was the most difficult job you've done?*

_____

_____

_____

_____

*Notes:*

# Work, Jobs, Money

*Have you ever owned your own business?*

*How did it start?*

*Who or what has been the most important help
to you in your work?*

*Notes:*

# Work, Jobs, Money

*What is the most extravagant
thing you've ever done?*

*Have you ever been caught in a
severe financial crisis?*

*Notes:*

# Work, Jobs, Money

*What do you think is the soundest*
*investment one can make?*

Notes:

# Family Lore

# Family Lore

*What were your grandparents' names?*

*Where did they come from?*
    *What did they do?*

*What memories do you have of them?*

*Who were your great aunts and uncles?*
    *Where did they live?*

*What did they do? What memories*
    *do you have of them?*

*Notes:*

## Family Lore

*What were/are your parents' names?*

_____

_____

_____

_____

*Where did/do they live?*

_____

_____

_____

*What did/do they do?*

_____

_____

_____

*What are your memories of the home
     you grew up in?*

_____

_____

_____

_____

*Notes:*

## Family Lore

*What are your thoughts about
    your mother?*

_____

_____

_____

*What are your thoughts about
    your father?*

_____

_____

_____

*What are the most important things
    you have learned from your father?*

_____

_____

_____

*What are the most important things
    you have learned from your mother?*

_____

_____

_____

*Notes:*

## Family Lore

*Do you have aunts and uncles?*

*What special thoughts do you have of them?*

*Do you have brothers and sisters?*
*How did/do you get along with them?*

*What did they look like when they were teenagers?*

*Notes:*

# Family Lore

*What work have they done?*

_____

_____

_____

*Where are they now?*

_____

_____

_____

*How far back can you trace your*
*mother's family?*

_____

_____

_____

*How far back can you trace your*
*father's family?*

_____

_____

_____

*Notes:*

## Family Lore

*Do we have any famous relatives?*
*Who? What have they done?*

_____

_____

*Who do you feel are our most successful*
*relatives? What have they accomplished?*

_____

_____

*Are there any characteristics which*
*you feel run through the family?*

_____

_____

_____

*Do you look more like your mother*
*or your father?*

_____

_____

_____

*Notes:*

## Family Lore

*Are there specific first names that
   are repeated through the family?*

*Have members of the family followed
   similar occupations or professions?*

*Have there been any exceptional athletes
   in the family?*

*Which relatives possess artistic talents?
   What?*

*Are there any medical problems
   that seem to run in the family?*

*Notes:*

# Family Lore

*Do we have any family legends?*

_____

_____

*What family traditions have we*
*always followed?*

_____

_____

*Are there any family "black sheep"?*
*Who are they? What did they do?*

_____

_____

_____

*Are there any curios or mementoes that*
*have been handed down over the years?*

_____

_____

_____

*Notes:*

## Family Lore

*Are there any family photographs or records? Where are they now?*

 

 

*Are there any favorite stories that are told and retold?*

 

 

 

 

 

*Who was the most beautiful woman in the family?*

 

*Who was the most handsome man in the family?*

 

*Notes:*

# Religion

# Religion

*Do you believe in God?*

_____

_____

_____

*Do you regularly attend a house of worship? Which one?*

_____

_____

_____

*Who is the first member of the clergy you recall? What was he like?*

_____

_____

*Has a member of the clergy had an influence on you? How?*

_____

_____

_____

*Did you attend a religious school? Which one? When?*

_____

_____

_____

*Notes:*

# Religion

*Did you ever want to become a
member of the clergy?*

*What is your favorite prayer?*

*What is your favorite religious music?*

*Are you active in social activities
(choral, fund raising, etc.) in your house of worship?*

*Notes:*

# Religion

*Is religion a major factor in your life?*

*How often do you read the Bible?*
*What is your favorite passage?*

*Do you interpret the Bible strictly*
*or loosely?*

*Notes:*

# Religion

*Have you ever explored other
    religions? Which ones? How?*

_____

_____

_____

*What was your most important
    religious experience?*

_____

_____

_____

_____

*Have you conducted any religious
    ceremonies in your home? What and when?*

_____

_____

_____

*What religious rituals or historic
    figures are most important to you?*

_____

_____

_____

_____

*Notes:*

# Religion

*How much religious training did you receive from your parents?*

*How much religious training did you give your children?*

*Have there been times when you questioned your religion? When and how?*

*How do you feel about prayers in schools?*

*Notes:*

# Religion

*Have there been times when your*
        *religion has helped you through difficult personal moments?*

*When?*

*What happened?*

*How do you feel about children*
        *being taught by members of religious orders?*

*Notes:*

# Religion

*At what period in your life has*
*       religion been most important to you?*

_____

_____

_____

_____

_____

_____

*Do you remember any bedtime prayers*
*       you said as a child? What were they?*

_____

_____

_____

_____

*Notes:*

# Some Favorite Things

# Some Favorite Things

*What are your favorite foods?*

*Drinks?*

*Animals?*

*Colors?*

*Places in the world?*

*Flowers?*

*Gifts to give?*

*Notes:*

## Some Favorite Things

*Gifts to receive?*

_____

_____

*Times of day?*

_____

_____

*Painting?*

_____

_____

*Sculpture?*

_____

_____

*Age?*

_____

_____

*Season?*

_____

_____

*Building?*

_____

*Notes:*

## Some Favorite Things

Magazines/Newspapers?

Authors?

Journalists?

Commentators?

Books?

Singers/Groups?

Orchestras/Bands?

Notes:

## Some Favorite Things

*Operas?*

*Symphonies?*

*Ballets?*

*Dances?*

*TV actors/actresses?*

*Notes:*

## Some Favorite Things

*TV shows?*

*Film actors/actresses?*

*Films?*

*Musicians?*

*Notes:*

## Some Favorite Things

*Radio programs?*

_____

_____

_____

*Comedians?*

_____

_____

_____

*Comic strips?*

_____

_____

_____

*Painters/Illustrators?*

_____

_____

_____

_____

*Notes:*

## Some Favorite Things

*Athletes?*

*Spectator sports?*

*Participant sports?*

*Sayings?*

*Notes:*

# Holidays
# and
# Traditions

# Holidays and Traditions

*What is your favorite holiday?*
  *What memories does it bring back?*

_____

_____

_____

*How do you observe it?*

_____

_____

_____

*What do you consider the most important*
  *family holidays?*

_____

_____

*Which family members have been*
  *responsible for hosting various holidays?*

_____

_____

_____

*Are there any traditional family foods?*

_____

_____

_____

*Notes:*

# Holidays and Traditions

*Are there any traditional family toasts?*

*Have you ever observed holidays of religions other than yours?*

*With whom?*
*Where?*

*Notes:*

# Holidays and Traditions

*What birthdays of family members
have been important celebrations?*

*What have been your best birthday parties?*

*What are the best gifts you've
ever received?*

*Notes:*

## Holidays and Traditions

*Did anyone ever have a surprise
    party for you?*

*What happened?*
*Were you really surprised?*

*What have been your most memorable
    wedding anniversaries?*

*Notes:*

## Holidays and Traditions

*Did your family gather together frequently?*
*Or just for the holidays?*

*What holiday traditions do you hope*
*I give to my own children?*

*Notes:*

# Pastimes, Hobbies, Collections

## Pastimes, Hobbies, Collections

*What do you most enjoy doing?*

*What talents or abilities have you
tried to develop?*

*Have you ever been on a stage?
What happened?*

*Have you ever had your name in a
newspaper? What paper? When and why?*

*Have you ever been on television?
When and why?*

*What type of books do you read most
often?*

*Notes:*

## Pastimes, Hobbies, Collections

*Have you ever won a drawing or a lottery? What did you win?*

*Have you gambled or made bets?*

*What have you bet on?*

*Do you play cards? What are your favorite card games?*

*Who are your favorite card partners?*

*Notes:*

# Pastimes, Hobbies, Collections

*Have you played musical instruments?*
*Which ones?*

_____

_____

_____

*How did you learn?*
*How long did you practice?*

_____

_____

_____

_____

_____

*What music did you play?*

_____

_____

_____

_____

*Notes:*

## Pastimes, Hobbies, Collections

*Have you collected things?*

*Stamps?*

*Coins?*

*Antiques?*

*Art?*

*Models?*

*Notes:*

# Pastimes, Hobbies, Collections

*Recipes?*

*Toys?*

*Books?*

*Records?*

*Other collectibles?*

*Where are your collections now?*

*Notes:*

## Pastimes, Hobbies, Collections

*Have you had other hobbies?*

*What organizations, clubs, or associations do you or have you belonged to?*

*What did they do?*

*How active have you been?*

*Notes:*

# Pastimes, Hobbies, Collections

*Have you been active in any charities
        as a volunteer?*

*What did you do?*

*What are your other interests?*

*Notes:*

# My Parent
# Your Child

# My Parent/Your Child

*When and where was my mother/father born?*
*How big was she/he?*

_____

_____

*Who delivered the baby?*

_____

_____

*Who was present?*

_____

_____

*Who were the first people you told?*

_____

_____

*How did you choose the name?*

_____

_____

*What was my parent like when she/*
*he was a small child?*

_____

_____

_____

*Notes:*

# My Parent/Your Child

*What were the first words my parent*
*ever spoke?*

_____

_____

*At what age did my parent take his/*
*her first steps?*

_____

_____

_____

*Were you a firm or easy-going*
*parent? How did he/she react?*

_____

_____

_____

_____

*Notes:*

## My Parent/Your Child

*What was his/her favorite entertainment
        as a teenager?*

_____

_____

_____

_____

_____

_____

_____

*What did my mother/father want to
        be when she/he grew up?*

_____

_____

_____

_____

_____

*Notes:*

# My Parent/Your Child

*What did you think she/he would
grow up to become?*

*What did she/he look like?*

*What did she /he do that made you
angry?*

*What did she/he do that made you
proud?*

Notes:

# My Parent/Your Child

*How was she/he as a student?*

*What clothes did she/he wear?*

*Did she/he ever get into trouble?*

*What chores did you make her/him do?*

*Notes:*

# My Parent/Your Child

*How much was her/his allowance?*

*Did she/he have a nickname?*
   *How did she/he get it?*

*What were her/his special talents?*

*What were her/his best habits?*

*Notes:*

# My Parent/Your Child

*What were her/his bad habits?*

_____

_____

_____

*Did she/he have a pet?*

_____

_____

_____

_____

*What did she/he want badly that you gave her/him?*

_____

_____

_____

*What did she/he talk about?*

_____

_____

_____

*Notes:*

# My Parent/Your Child

*What were the most difficult
    questions she/he asked?*

_____

_____

_____

*Who in the family did she/he resemble?*

_____

_____

_____

*What did you find most difficult
    to allow her/him to do?*

_____

_____

_____

*How did you meet your future son/
    daughter-in-law (my father/mother)?*

_____

_____

_____

*Notes:*

## My Parent/Your Child

*What did you think?*

*What did you have to say?*

*Did you feel they would get married?*

*Tell me about my parents' wedding.*

*Notes:*

# History
# and
# Politics

# History and Politics

*To which political party do you belong? Why?*

*Which national candidates have you
    voted for over the years?*

*Which local candidates have you
    backed over the years?*

*Have you worked in a political campaign?
    For Whom?*

*When?*
*What did you do?*

*Notes:*

## History and Politics

*What do you feel government does well?*

_____

_____

_____

_____

_____

_____

_____

_____

*What do you feel government does badly?*

_____

_____

_____

_____

_____

_____

_____

_____

*Notes:*

# History and Politics

*What is your most vivid historical memory?*

_____

_____

_____

_____

*What world events have most affected*
*    your life?*

_____

_____

_____

*What inventions or technological advances have*
*    most changed your life? How?*

_____

_____

_____

*Notes:*

## History and Politics

*What national events have most
affected your life?*

_____

_____

_____

_____

_____


*What local events have affected
your life?*

_____

_____

_____

_____

_____

_____

_____

*Notes:*

## History and Politics

*What causes or issues do you now feel
 strongly about?*

*What causes or issues have you felt
 strongly about in the past?*

*Notes:*

# Between Us

## Between Us

*What are you most proud of doing?*

*What are you most proud of being?*

*Notes:*

## Between Us

*Have you ever gone to a psychiatrist
or a psychologist?*

*What do you think about therapy?*

*What do you think about using them?*

*What was your most exciting experience?*

*Notes:*

## Between Us

*What was your happiest experience?*

_____

_____

_____

_____

_____

_____

_____

*What was your saddest experience?*

_____

_____

_____

_____

_____

_____

_____

*Notes:*

# Between Us

*What goals have you set for your future?*

_____

_____

_____

_____

_____

_____

*What do you hope the future holds for me?*

_____

_____

_____

_____

_____

_____

*Notes:*

## Between Us

*Whom do you love? What do you love?*

*Notes:*

## Memorabilia

*Photographs, Clippings, Cards, Letters*

## Memorabilia

*Photographs, Clippings, Cards, Letters*

## Memorabilia

*Photographs, Clippings, Cards, Letters*

## Memorabilia

*Photographs, Clippings, Cards, Letters*

## Memorabilia

*Photographs, Clippings, Cards, Letters*

## Memorabilia

*Photographs, Clippings, Cards, Letters*

## Memorabilia

*Photographs, Clippings, Cards, Letters*

## Memorabilia

*Photographs, Clippings, Cards, Letters*

A
Grandparents
Book

# Family Tree

Great-
Grandmother

Great-
Grandmother

Great-
Grandfather

Grandmother

Grandfather

Mother

*See inside of front cover for additional family tree. Two trees are provided so both Grandfather and Grandmother's family names can be recorded.*